ICONS
OF
STYLE

# SNEAKERS

MITCHELL BEAZLEY

# SNEAKERS

**The**
# DAILY
# STREET

# Contents

Whatever you want to call them – trainers, sneakers, kicks, crepes – each person has their own take on what makes a shoe design a style icon. Whether you're an avid sneaker collector or an obsessive for the technical aspects of sports shoe design, or just someone who likes a select few designs, there are always going to be certain shoes that remain timeless and achieve success across the generations.

Sports shoes – or sneakers as we'll call them for the purpose of this book – have become a powerful symbol worldwide. Wearing a specific design communicates a personal aesthetic, attitude and knowledge to those who share the same interests. It's a unique way of connecting with like-minded people, acting as a sort of code that can communicate knowledge and appreciation for design, an affinity for a certain time period, a connection to a certain subculture, an awareness of the latest trend … or simply a love for a comfortable shoe. It's something that originally started out relatively small, enjoyed and understood by a tiny minority, but of late it has boomed into a multimillion-dollar industry, one that doesn't show any signs of slowing down.

The landscape of collecting sports shoes significantly changed over the decade of 2000–2010, mostly thanks to the advance of the Internet. What was once a monthly or bimonthly schedule has become a weekly barrage, offering consumers a seemingly endless wealth of models, colourways, materialways, hybrids and innovations on classic silhouettes – not to mention all the new silhouette designs and future classics being created.

# Introduction

Many books have covered the obsession with collecting sneakers, but in this book we aim to document the iconic shoe designs of the past and present decades that have had a specific impact on the evolution of sports shoe style. We hope that it will serve as an objective reminder of how this culture was built up and where it came from, and as an indicator of where it is today. We hope, too, that *Sneakers* will also serve as a reference book – both for those who are new to the obsession with buying sports shoes and for more seasoned collectors who might just stumble across an iconic design that sparks their interest further.

One of the joys of sneaker collecting and sports shoe fanaticism is that it comes down to personal taste and opinion. This is certainly not a book on the 'best sneakers ever made', nor is it some dictatorial list of what you *ought* to like. It's a book containing 50 sneaker silhouettes that have had some of the largest impacts on style – whether this was at the time of their release, or later on in their career. There are even a few designs here whose full impact, we feel, is yet to be seen.

Let's be honest: for some the world of sneakers remains a strange subculture, but we hope that this book will shine a light on the influence that sneakers have had on fashion, style and culture over the decades – and will continue to have over decades to come.

Few shoe designs cross the boundaries within fashion like the Converse Chuck Taylor, a true footwear and style icon. Originally released in 1917, the familiar 'All Star' name would be followed in 1923 by the Chuck Taylor name tag. The name addition paid homage to Charles 'Chuck' Taylor, a world-renowned basketball player and Converse salesman of the time who made a few alterations to the original 1917 All Star design.

Walk down most streets and it's pretty much guaranteed that you will spot someone wearing a pair of 'Chucks' in one of the many versions available. Their wide availability has allowed for generation after generation across the world to adopt this classic shoe as its own. The beauty of the Chuck Taylor All Star is that it has pretty much ended up in most fashion and subcultural circles in some way or another.

In the 1970s new colour options took over the originals for a short while and attracted a whole new audience. Those '70s versions have made a comeback more recently through a string of much-anticipated reissues. The shoe has been favoured in the music, sports and fashion worlds for decades. Still to this day you'll find the shoe worn by many in a diverse range of social groups including the punk, rock 'n' roll, pop and hip-hop scenes.

Opposite: Few shoe designs have truly gained success like the Chuck Taylor All Star, even after its 90-plus years of existence.

9

# Converse Chuck Taylor All Star

1923

Recent reissues
have seen a
revival of the
details found on
the Chuck Taylor
All Stars of the
1970s.

# Converse
# Jack Purcell

1935

In 1935 the undefeated world badminton champion John Edward 'Jack' Purcell designed a badminton shoe for the B F Goodrich Company with the aim of creating a shoe that offered more protection and support on court. Jack Purcell had an enviable reputation, holding the world championship title from 1933 to 1945, when he finally retired from the sport. It's a reputation that would be hard to equal, but his shoe has gone on to well and truly surpass it, with the name Jack Purcell now being more closely associated with the shoe than with a successful sporting career.

In 1972 Converse purchased the trademark rights to the Jack Purcell shoe from B F Goodrich, adding the already iconic sneaker to its roster, alongside the equally iconic Converse Chuck Taylor All Star (see pages 8–11). Over the decades the Jack Purcell may have taken a step back from the limelight, having been eclipsed by the Converse All Star, but it has remained a firm favourite among the more sartorially minded thanks to its mature aesthetic and reduced marketing push. Its trademark 'smile' on the toe box makes this sneaker instantly recognizable and it continues to be a classic in menswear as well as in other style categories.

Opposite and below: The Jack Purcell has found its home in menswear, but has also gained recognition from streetwear greats such as Undefeated.

# adidas
# Samba

1950

The adidas Samba is a sporting icon. Designed in the late 1940s and first released in 1950, the Samba was created for use on cold, icy ground, allowing footballers (soccer players) to train with more traction in winter. Hard to believe now, but the gum outsole on the Samba was an original innovation in 1950, and thanks to its traction the Samba became *the* indoor football (soccer) shoe, too, dominating the market until the 1990s when rival brands finally got in on the action.

In the 1970s the adidas Samba was reinterpreted by the UK association football fan subculture known as the Football Casuals, becoming part of the uniform worn by fans of English clubs. It's a look that's gone on to be iconic in its own right, with the Samba still one of the staple pairs.

Outside of football and football (soccer) culture, the Samba has proven a popular choice in many fashion and style circles thanks to its classic looks and sleek shape. It has won adherents among skateboarders, too, becoming the main inspiration behind the adidas Skateboarding Busenitz shoe.

You can't talk about sneaker culture in Europe without mentioning the Football Casuals, and you can't talk about the Football Casuals without mentioning the adidas Samba. It's an icon and for good reasons – it introduced gum outsoles (a much loved part of sneakers for most enthusiasts) and helped to secure adidas at a point when the brand was still getting on to its feet after World War II.

Opposite and below: Since its inception in 1950 the Samba has changed quite substantially but still retains a lot of its original appeal.

# Vans
# Authentic

In 1966 Paul Van Doren and his three business partners opened the doors of the first Van Doren Rubber Company shop in California, launching with only three styles of shoes, all manufactured around the corner, in their own factory. One of these original three silhouettes was what we now know as the Authentic but which was originally billed as the #44. The Authentic was designed as a deck shoe, with no notion of it becoming the icon that it's become for all kinds of subcultures, most specifically skateboarding.

In the early days of the Van Doren Rubber Company, the shoes were made to order direct from the California-based store. As time passed, fans of the brand took it upon themselves to abbreviate the rather long name, giving it the snappier billing that we all know it by now – Vans. In a similar fashion, local kids in the early 1970s started using the Vans deck shoe for skateboarding, thereby firmly attaching the shoe and the brand to skate culture from the start.

Spotting a growing market and a potential shift in market direction, Vans invited pro skateboarders Tony Alva and Stacy Peralta to design a shoe specifically for skateboarding. This was the moment in 1975 when the Authentic was tweaked and reinterpreted as the Era (originally known as the #95) – the first skate shoe had been born.

Today the Vans Authentic continues to be one of the most iconic sneakers ever created and is the preferred footwear for all kinds of subcultures throughout the world, making it one of Vans's best-selling shoes.

Opposite: Vans would go on to become the first skateboarding shoe brand, tweaking the Authentic to create the first skate shoe.

# PUMA
# Suede

1968

One of the all-time style icons and one of PUMA's exemplary designs, few shoes have the rich history and cultural relevance of the PUMA Suede. Its simple design, durable materials and multiple colour options continue to appeal to each new generation.

Originally released in 1968, the Suede is also known as the PUMA States. A close relation, the PUMA Clyde is – apart from minor design changes – essentially a Suede, taking its name from basketball star Walter 'Clyde' Frazier. The PUMA Basket is a slightly wider and leather version of the PUMA Suede.

The Suede, along with the adidas Superstar (see pages 20–3), was originally a basketball shoe but was also a must-have for B-boys in the 1970s and 1980s. The PUMA Suede has played a huge role in street fashion, its bold colour options matched up with other key items of an outfit to create a strong personal style. Lace colour and width were also an important factor when styling the shoe. Many B-boys would use fat laces and matching coloured variants to communicate their style. Because the shoe was designed with basketball in mind, it actually provided B-boys with performance attributes too, aiding their dance skills.

In the 1990s a plethora of new colour options were made available and the shoe's popularity among collectors was revived and refreshed, though interest also came from newcomers. The enduring appeal of the Suede is that it pretty much goes with any look and style.

Opposite and below: Originally a basketball shoe, the PUMA Suede has been embraced by many different subcultures, from B-boys to skateboarders.

The Superstar was the low version of the adidas Pro Model. Originally released in 1969, the shoe had a unique design feature in the form of its rubber toe box, which was later responsible for the Superstar's 'Shell Toe' moniker.

The first colourways were simple affairs, with accents in black, white, navy and red. As a performance shoe, the Superstar was designed to play basketball in, but in the 1980s renowned hip-hop artists started to adopt the shoe for its styling and fit. Most notably, rap group Run–D.M.C. would help the Superstar achieve iconic status through their endorsement of the shoe, which led to one of the group's best-known tracks, My adidas. The group's personal take on the Superstar involved the removal of the laces, which exposed the tongue and foregrounded the shoe's chunky silhouette. All of this led to a line of Run–D.M.C. adidas apparel and shoes. The demand for the Superstar exploded.

Over the years there have been many collaborations using the Superstar. The Japanese clothing imprint A Bathing Ape would create some of the most popular limited-edition versions of the shoe, as did other streetwear stalwarts such as Undefeated, Atmos and CLOT. More recently, adidas released the adidas Superstar '80s, which has replenished enthusiasm for the shoe and its heritage.

Opposite:     21
Hip-hop group
Run–D.M.C.
would help
to rocket the
Superstar,
along with the
adidas brand, to
super-stardom.

# adidas
# Superstar

1969

From humble
beginnings the
adidas Superstar
would go on to
become one of
the most instantly
recognizable shoes
in the world.

# Nike
# Cortez

1972

Founded by Phil Knight and invested in by Bill Bowerman, Nike began life as Blue Ribbon Sports (BRS), the distributor for Onitsuka Tiger running shoes in the United Sates. During the BRS representation era of 1964–71 Bill Bowerman tweaked Onitsuka Tiger's running shoes, making them more specific for the needs of the Western physique. Released in 1968 for the Mexico City Olympics and exclusive to the US market, the Onitsuka Tiger Cortez took the running world by storm.

While still operating BRS, Phil Knight and Bill Bowerman started their own sports brand named Nike and started manufacturing the Cortez with the now-famous Swoosh logo on it instead of the Onitsuka stripes. The story goes that it wasn't until an Onitsuka Tiger official visited the BRS warehouse in Los Angeles, and bumped into a pair of Nike Cortez shoes, that Onitsuka Tiger found out what was going on. Eventually, the two companies went their separate ways. After a court hearing declared that both brands could continue to produce the same shoe, Nike stuck with the Cortez name while Onitsuka Tiger renamed it the Corsair. It's the only time that a shoe has been a bestseller for two different brands.

The Nike Cortez was officially first released in 1972, changing the world for ever as Nike entered the market. However, it wasn't until Nike dropped the rubber toe reinforcement in the mid-1970s that the world saw the Cortez as we know it today. It's hard to think that there was a time where there was no Nike in sports, but before the Cortez that time existed. Through forward-thinking marketing and product development, Nike would go on to dominate the running market and the Cortez played a very large part in that. Outside of running, the Cortez sparked a fascination with the Swoosh logo, going on to make its now-iconic appearance in the 1994 classic film *Forrest Gump*.

Opposite: The beginning of the Nike brand: the 1972 Cortez remains one of the most significant sneakers of all time.

The Nike Blazer was one of Nike's earliest basketball shoes, characterized by the big-bellied Nike Swoosh on the side profile that emphasized the shoe's hi-top cut.

The Blazer was championed by basketball legends George Gervin, aka 'The Iceman', and Geoff Petrie. The shoe was appropriately named, however, after the NBA team Portland Trailblazers (Nike's hometown). Like the Nike Dunk (see pages 50–1), the Nike Blazer regained collectors' attention in the early 2000s owing to collaborative efforts from the likes of streetwear subbrand Stüssy. The collaboration resulted in two colourways that are among some of the rarest versions of the Blazer. Materials used on the Blazer usually consist of leather, suede and mesh.

Since the first reissues, the Blazer has achieved mainstream success with the low- and high-cut vintage variations. These presented both the original colours and new variations in a reworked vintage style that emulated a dated Nike Blazer from the 1970s. Initial responses within collecting circles were positive and the Blazer Vintage soon went on to achieve success at a mainstream level, opening up the sneaker market further, as musicians and celebrities sported the new vintage editions.

Opposite: One of Nike's earliest basketball shoe designs, the Nike Blazer regained popularity in the early 2000s.

27

# Nike Blazer

1973

# adidas
# Trimm Trab

1975

First released in 1975, the adidas Trimm Trab was originally designed as a fitness and training shoe. A decade later the design became a must-have for football (soccer) fans and soon became a stadium classic in England. To this day, hardcore adidas fans revere the Trimm Trab.

High-quality materials were used to construct the simple design, with suede and a dual-density sole unit. After the initial release, the Trimm Trab 2 followed in 1984 and the Trimm Star in 1985. Other adidas models in the 1970s and 1980s would continue to be inspired by the Trimm Trab, including classics such as the Centre Court, Madrid and München. They would use the original PU sole unit, which was revolutionary at the time owing to its flexibility, shock absorption, excellent grip and lightweight feel.

The shoe initially re-attained popularity back in 2004 after 12 variations of the Trimm Trab were reissued, with further releases this side of 2010. The Argentina Blue variations are favoured by many long-term adidas collectors. A limited edition Liverpool version was released to commemorate the opening of an adidas store in Liverpool, England in 2007, with only 100 pairs produced.

Opposite and below: A classic adidas shoe design and still a fan favourite in countries such as England, the Trimm Trab was a simple design constructed with quality materials.

# Vans
# Old Skool

1977

The Vans Old Skool was first introduced in 1977, with its original Style #36 'Off The Wall' name tag. It followed in the footsteps of the Vans Era and incorporated many of the same features, including the cushioned insole, arc support, padded collar, reinforced heel and the famous waffle outsole. However, the Old Skool took Vans's shoes to a new level, with the original versions featuring a leather toe cap and leather heel as well as the distinctive Vans side stripe.

Earlier versions of the Old Skool had a slightly different shape to the reissues we see today, with the originals featuring a smaller toe cap and being made available in narrow, medium and wide fits. Vans's use of durable quality materials such as leather and suede made the Old Skool a must-have for skateboarders, while its unique design and bold colours appealed to a wider audience, too. The shoe was also endorsed by many legendary skaters including Stacy Peralta, Tony Alva and Geoff Rowley.

The Old Skool has a rich history in American West Coast fashion and continues to be a shoe of choice in many subcultures. More specifically, the shoe was a favourite in the US punk and hardcore movements, which led to special versions of the Old Skool being created with bands such as Bad Religion, Circle Jerks and the Descendents. Even with the widespread appeal of Vans today, the Old Skool still remains a favourite in skateboarding and other countercultures.

Opposite: From being a huge success on the West Coast skateboarding scene to being appreciated throughout Europe, the Vans Old Skool is a timeless classic.

# adidas
# Stan Smith

1978

One of the most iconic sneakers ever created, the Stan Smith as we know it was released in 1978, though its exact origins are a little cloudy.

Rewind to 1964 and this tennis shoe was originally the pro model for French tennis player Robert Haillet and was the first ever leather tennis shoe. On Haillet's retirement from tennis in 1971, adidas reassigned the adidas Robert Haillet shoe to American tennis player Stan Smith, not wanting to drop what was already a very successful shoe for the brand. Strangely, adidas kept Robert Haillet as the shoe name, adding the now-famous Endorsed by Stan Smith branding to the tongue along with Stan Smith's grinning face. To resolve this confusing situation, adidas renamed the shoe the adidas Stan Smith in 1978, slightly tweaking the shape and heel tab to create the Stan Smith that we know and love today.

Outside of tennis, this is one of the most successful sports shoes ever designed. It has transcended multiple generations and subcultures without losing any relevance or style appeal, and isn't showing any signs of slowing down. Having been removed from store shelves in 2012, adidas relaunched the Stan Smith at the beginning of 2014 as part of a large-scale global operation, once again breathing new life into this enduring classic.

Opposite and below: These archive originals have a few different details on them compared to the Stan Smiths we know today.

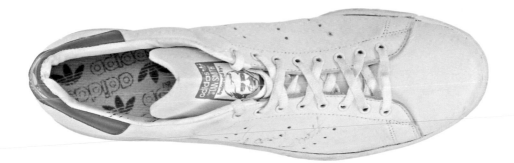

When considering a brand with such a rich heritage, it is hard to pinpoint specific key moments in its development. Nonetheless, the issue of the Slip-On (originally known as the #98) stands out as one of the most important turning-points for Vans, and for a couple of reasons.

Created in 1979, the sneaker's simple design was welcomed by skateboarders and surfers alike, principally on account of the vast amount of blank canvas on the shoe's upper. This allowed kids to customize their Slip-Ons by drawing on them, and one particular trend came through – checkerboard. Again quick to spot an opportunity, Vans started printing the checkerboard on to their Slip-Ons. In 1982 the checkerboard pattern was given a further boost thanks to Sean Penn's character Jeff Spicoli who wears the sneakers in the film *Fast Times at Ridgemont High*. This put Vans – and the checkerboard pattern the company is now so strongly tied to – on the global stage.

Like many iconic Vans models, the Slip-On has been reinterpreted again and again by all kinds of people and in all kinds of styles.

Opposite and below: The Vans Slip-On was always more than a shoe: it was a blank canvas and a symbol of a generation.

35

# Vans Slip-On

1979

Like many other early adidas models, the Campus has stood the test of time and has continued to be a fan favourite among musicians, collectors and the general public. The Campus started life as the Tournament in the early 1970s, before some design tweaks and a name change in 1980.

Like the Superstar (see pages 20–3), the adidas Campus had strong links to the New York City hip-hop scene in the 1980s. Most famously, the shoe was associated with the Beastie Boys, even featuring on the cover of their 1992 album *Check Your Head*. It was also the shoe of choice, among other adidas classics, for B-boys. Its lightweight feel and low cut allowed for maximum movement. The adaptation of the Campus by breakdancers inspired skateboarders to adopt the shoe, too, drawn by the benefits of the hardwearing suede and the range of colourways available. No doubt taking its cue from this, adidas today produces a skateboarding version of the Campus.

Over more recent years, adidas provided a new variation of the shoe with the Campus 80s, which has a slimmer silhouette and stripped-back details. This new design has been harnessed by Japanese designer Kazuki Kuraishi (aka KZK), who has created many new and collectible editions of the Campus 80s model. The relationship between the brand and Kuraishi has also resulted in limited-edition adidas apparel collections. Other notable collaboration partners using the adidas Campus include Footpatrol, Mita, A Bathing Ape (BAPE) and Neighborhood. More recently, the Campus has also seen a Primeknit version – the first adidas Originals silhouette to get the Primeknit makeover.

Opposite: The Campus has remained a timeless classic for the adidas brand, respected by some of fashion and streetwear's biggest names.

37

# adidas Campus

1980

# Saucony
# Jazz Original

**1981**

At the time of its release in 1981, the Jazz Original was one of Saucony's most technical running shoes. When designing the shoe, Saucony worked with renowned Boston sports podiatrist Frank Santopietro, introducing new technologies such as the Maxitrac outsole, Butterfly Balancing design and Saucony sock insert to create a running shoe that focused on weight (or lack of it) and balance.

Fast-forward to 1998 and the Jazz Original had long been retired as old technology. However, it was that year that Saucony decided to revisit its archives, re-releasing the Jazz Original under a new subbrand named Saucony Originals for the more price-conscious running enthusiast. It proved a decisive move. By 1999 Saucony Originals accounted for a third of the company's net sales and the brand saw its stock prices more than triple in value.

Having been a large reason why Saucony was loved by runners in the early 1980s, the Saucony Jazz Original was once again contributing to the future of the brand, helping it to move into the lifestyle market and to penetrate the world of fashion. The Saucony Jazz Original still remains one of the brand's key styles.

Opposite:
The Saucony branding may be different, but the Jazz Original itself remains nearly unchanged in modern reissues, keeping its classic appeal.

First released in 1982, it didn't take too long for the Air Force 1 to achieve success both on and off the basketball court. It was the first Nike basketball shoe to feature a full-length Nike Air sole unit, which provided basketball players with improved technical support and performance.

The hi-top version of the Air Force 1, with its ankle strap, provided unprecedented ankle support. Combined with the lacing system, the strap created a lockdown support system for the foot. That same ankle strap would also be reinterpreted by those wearing the Air Force 1 for fashion purposes. That 'off-court' style would also re-enter the professional basketball world through the likes of NBA star Rasheed Wallace, who continued playing in 'AF1s' way into the late 2000s.

The hip-hop scene and New York City's love affair with the shoe would further solidify the Air Force 1 as a streetwear essential. A huge number of colour variations have been made available since its original release, not to mention a large number of high-profile collaborations and limited-edition versions, enabling the Air Force 1 to retain its special character and appeal over three decades. Among other hybrids, the Air Force 1 was reinvented as the Lunar Force 1 in 2012 and was updated again in 2014, ensuring that this classic continues to be a product of innovation.

Opposite: The Air Force 1 continues to be one of the most coveted shoe designs of all time. The low-, mid- and hi-top versions continue to be a success.

# Nike
# Air Force 1

**1982**

# Reebok 🇬🇧 FITNESS

## HI-TOP FREESTYLE

In 1983 a British sportswear brand would change the sneaker world for ever. Reebok created a shoe specifically aimed at the burgeoning new 'fitness' market, using glove leather (aka garment leather) to create a supple shoe for women's aerobics. This was the first time a fitness shoe had been designed specifically for women. While other brands failed to take the fitness movement seriously at this time, Reebok spotted its potential and proceeded to dominate what would become a huge market.

The Freestyle Hi was the hi-top version of Reebok's Freestyle, also launched in 1982, and was originally called the Reebok Hi-Top Freestyle, although many people called the shoe simply the '54.11' after the price of the sneaker in US dollars. The Freestyle Hi is an iconic shoe not only for Reebok but for the 1980s and sportswear more generally, symbolizing the start of the fitness movement and the beginnings of Reebok's use of garment leather to create all-white leather sneakers (see pages 44–5).

The Freestyle Hi has enjoyed several resurgences in popularity, never truly disappearing from the limelight, but having particular moments such as the big Freestyle revival in 2009 among young women.

Opposite: The advert shown here sums up how Reebok pitched the Freestyle Hi shoe as the future of the 1980s fitness trend.

# Reebok Freestyle Hi

1982

This is most likely the sneaker that Reebok will forever be remembered for. Although by no means its earliest running shoe (Reebok had started making running shoes as early as 1958 and, under the J W Foster & Sons name, as far back as 1895), the Reebok Classic Leather has undoubtedly had the most impact on style and culture.

At a time when sportswear companies were avoiding the use of leather for running shoes owing to its stiffness, Reebok applied its soft garment leather, first brought to the market on its Freestyle shoes in 1982 (see pages 42–3), to a running shoe design and birthed the Reebok Classic Leather. It is worth noting that a suede and nylon version, simply called the Reebok Classic, was also released in 1983, though it was quickly outshone by its leather sibling

The Classic Leather was always destined to become a style icon, having originally been designed with style-conscious men and women in mind and targeting itself at the fitness-obsessed generation of the 1980s. Over the decades the Reebok Classic Leather has remained a timeless classic and one of the most revered shoe designs in history, becoming a popular choice for all sorts of subcultures, especially in the UK where it is viewed as a British classic.

Opposite: The Reebok Classic Leather has always been a firm favourite in Britain. More recently, it has enjoyed a revived popularity thanks to its clean looks.

# Reebok
# Classic Leather

1983

Originally designed for the 1984 Los Angeles Olympics, the adidas LA Trainer achieved huge success as a running shoe throughout the 1980s and also went on to become a retro style icon.

The LA Trainer was a lightweight running shoe made from an attractive combination of nylon mesh and suede on the upper. It also pioneered a brand-new adidas technology – the Vario Shock Absorption System – featuring pegs in the heel that, to a degree, allowed the wearer to control the level of cushioning. The innovation proved a success for adidas, finding its way into other future classics such as the Grand Slam and Keglar. One of the other most recognizable features of the shoe is the foil LA Trainer branding on the stripe closest to the heel, a motif that was added to the design only in 1989.

Debuting at the Los Angeles Olympics, the LA Trainer became a global success and has gone on to become one of adidas's most recognizable models, ageing beautifully as a design for fashion and style.

Opposite and below: Over the years the L.A. Trainer has undergone a few design tweaks, including some simplification of the panels surrounding the toe box.

# adidas LA Trainer

1984

The adidas ZX 500 was first released in 1984 as part of the ZX '00 family, providing a balanced cross between a trail and running shoe. The mix of mesh, suede and nylon was forward-thinking and set the tone for adidas running shoes for years after. The support and breathability on the upper was complemented by its TPU counter and EVA midsole, which helped to keep the right balance when in motion. It was the perfect blend of considered materials and technology.

In 2002 reissues of the model started to appear – a programme that carried on throughout the 2000s, with an array of strong colourways. The appeal of the ZX 500 as a lifestyle shoe soon became apparent. Even among other established 1980s and 1990s runners, the ZX 500 still resonates with collectors and sports shoe fans.

In 2008 the appeal of the ZX 500 was also helped by the outstanding adidas Consortium AZX project, that saw the brand collaborating with a huge number of subbrands from around the world for their take on the ZX range. Associates included the likes of Colette, D-mop, Footpatrol, Crooked Tongues and Patta.

Modern updates of the ZX 500 include the Weave versions, which reintroduced the shoe to a modern audience and also helped reshape the shoe's aesthetics and appeal. The original ZX 500 colourway of grey and red still remains one of adidas's best-loved colour palettes.

Opposite: The ZX 500 was a running shoe design ahead of its time. The stylish mix of mesh, suede and nylon has fuelled the shoe's appeal.

# adidas
# ZX 500

1984

Before the introduction of the Air Jordan I to the NBA courts, the Nike Dunk was the go-to choice for basketball players, and for those off the basketball court as well. In 1985 Nike released the Dunk in a variety of different colourways. During the 1985–6 basketball tournaments held by the National Collegiate Athletic Association (NCAA), college teams such as Syracuse, Michigan and Arizona State selected the Dunk as their shoe to play in. Owing to the number of colour options, each university could easily match up its team colours to the shoes. Even the Nike Dunk shoe box matched the colour scheme of the shoe.

In 1998 Nike reissued the Dunk, to the relief of many long-term fans of the shoe. Since then, the Dunk has achieved huge success and received lots of attention, especially in the early to mid-2000s. The design was subject to many high-profile collaborations, including projects with Supreme and Jeff Staple, and was also produced in new colourways, both of which resulted in a Dunk collecting frenzy.

The Nike Dunk also contributed to Nike's future success within the skateboarding industry. With its extra-padded tongue, durable materials and limited-edition colourways, the Dunk SB was a huge success among both skaters and collectors.

Opposite: The Nike Dunk has gone from being a basketball favourite to a skateboarder's choice, and finally to a streetwear classic.

# Nike Dunk

1985

Designed for basketball legend Michael Jordan by Peter Moore at Nike, the Air Jordan I was the beginning of the long-running Nike Air Jordan signature line. Despite its success, it had a controversial start.

Michael Jordan got to wear the black/red version only three times on the court before the National Basketball Association (NBA) stepped in and banned the shoe. Why? Simply because the shoe broke the NBA league colour regulations. Nike couldn't have wished for more. What better way to fuel interest in a shoe than for it to be banned? Nike continued to pay the $5,000 fine every time Jordan stepped on to the court with the colourful Air Jordan I on his feet. Although collecting sports shoes had long been a craze in metropolitan areas like New York City, the banning of the black/red Air Jordans created a frenzy and also sparked interest in collecting sports shoes further afield. The Air Jordan I marked the beginning of 'sneaker collecting' as we know it today.

The design itself was revolutionary and bold, too. Now known as the 'Banned' (Nike would later reissue a version in 2011 that played on this idea) or 'Breds', the design utilized premium leather, a striking red colour and the winged basketball Air Jordan logo. Later, a version with white accents was released that proved just as popular.

Other fan favourites to this day include the black/royal and black toe versions, among an array of other colour options. With its ankle protection and durability, the Air Jordan I has found popularity among skateboarders and was recently released under the Nike SB skateboarding brand. That crossover appeal still stays strong today, with the shoe worn with various styles.

Opposite:
The banned colourway, combined with the allure of Michael Jordan's exciting style of play, contributed to the Air Jordan I's huge success.

# Nike
# Air Jordan I

1985

Signing Michael Jordan and giving him his own signature line would prove to be one of the most important decisions Nike ever made.

The Air Max 1 is yet another key moment in Nike history and one of Tinker Hatfield's greatest designs, aided by the then-developer Mark Parker. Although Tinker was not the designer of Nike's Air technology (that honour goes to Frank Rudy in 1977, who debuted it in the Nike 'Tailwind' of 1978), it is his Air Max 1 with its 'visible air' window in the midsole that made people wake up to Air technology.

Inspired by the 'inside-out' architecture of the Pompidou Centre in Paris, Tinker Hatfield had the idea of showing people the Air technology in Nike shoes by cutting a 'window' into the midsole of the Air Max 1. To focus further attention on this feature, Tinker created a bright-red frame on the upper that drew the eye to the white midsole. At the time, it was a daring move to use such a bright colour palette, especially for a non-racing shoe, and there were a lot of people at Nike who didn't believe the Air Max 1 would be a success. After a long process of design, development and testing, the Air Max 1 was released in 1987, alongside the Nike Air Safari (see pages 58–9) and Air Trainer, thereby changing running, Nike and sneakers for good, and starting one of Nike's best-loved running shoe lines.

Since its creation, the Air Max 1 has gone on to become one of the most iconic shoe designs of all time, often used as a symbol for sneaker culture as a whole. Over the decades various high-profile collaborations and technical innovations have helped to ensure that the Air Max 1 remains relevant and continues to capture attention. Although the technology has long been surpassed, the love for this shoe isn't showing any signs of fading.

Opposite: The Air Max 1 was a revolution in sneaker design, from its window in the midsole to its use of bold colours.

# Nike
# Air Max 1

1987

# Nike
# Air Safari

1987

Originally designed by Tinker Hatfield for running and track sports in 1987, the Nike Air Safari utilized a unique mix of luxury materials and aesthetics. Its leather upper is complemented by distinctive speckled grey panels, which have since become synonymous with the model. Back in the late 1980s, however, its bright-orange accents proved to be a controversial aesthetic for an athlete's shoe.

The Air Safari was part of the 1987 Air Pack, which otherwise comprised the Air Max 1 (see pages 56–7), Air Trainer 1, Air Sock and Air Revolution – all now iconic designs. The Air Safari's performance was matched by its luxurious aesthetic and materials, allowing the shoe to also be worn for casual purposes. One of the unique features of the Air Safari was its safari print, inspired, it's said, by high-end furniture and the luxurious materials used to construct it, such as ostrich skin. Its use of quality materials, found throughout the shoe, is one of the contributing factors to the design's cult status within the sneaker collecting community.

The design didn't receive widespread attention until Nike presented reissues of the model in 2003. Its unique speckled pattern would gain further popularity through a special collaboration between Atmos and Nike, where the pattern was utilized on the Air Max 1. This inspired further use of the Safari speckle on other Nike models in the years that followed, creating further appreciation of the Air Safari original.

Opposite and below: The unique grey speckled panels and orange accents of the Air Safari were mixed with luxury materials to produce a running shoe way ahead of its time.

Originally designed for running and released in 1988, the New Balance 574 was constructed of quality materials and featured the brand's ENCAP system in the midsole. ENCAP technology provided stability and shock absorption and was a feature on many other running designs from the brand. The 574 was produced in a variety of different materials, with full leather or suede and mesh variations available.

In 2003 New Balance reissued the 574, which came in new colour options and material combinations. Since then, the 574 has developed from an underrated collectors' gem to a menswear and unisex fashion favourite. New Balance's running designs from the 1980s and 1990s have become increasingly popular in menswear across the globe. The Made In England and Made In USA editions are of particular interest to both collectors and menswear enthusiasts owing to the use of premium materials, limited runs and original colourways. Various collaboration efforts with Concepts, UBIQ, Undefeated and Mita have further solidified the 574 as a connoisseur's shoe of choice.

New Balance continues to execute its archive designs in a way that appeals to a quality-conscious audience. That attention to detail and quality production values have allowed New Balance shoes, and more specifically the 574, to grow in popularity. The 574 has become a firm favourite and continues to prove its timeless design and appeal.

Opposite: The New Balance 574 continues to be a huge success in fashion circles and among those attentive to quality and detail.

# New Balance 574

1988

# Nike
# Air Jordan III

1988

Designed by Tinker Hatfield, the Air Jordan III was a ground-breaking shoe in many respects. Not only was it an innovative design for the Nike Air Jordan signature line, it also set the standard for basketball shoe design in the years that followed.

The Air Jordan III was released in 1988 and was the first to showcase the new Jumpman logo. Replacing the winged logo used on the Air Jordan I (see pages 52–5) and Air Jordan II, the Jumpman design was instantly recognizable, acting as a hallmark of quality for players and shoe collectors alike. Although original versions of the Air Jordan III used the Nike Air logo on the heel, modern reissues have mostly replaced this with the Jumpman. However, more recently the Nike Air logo was temporarily put back in place, much to the satisfaction of collectors.

Another vital design element of the shoe was the introduction of the now-famous elephant print. This material opened doors into the fashion world and solidified the Air Jordan III as a legitimate fashion product as well as a shoe with a functional design. This combination of fashion and function was integral to the success of the Air Jordan signature line as well as to the models that followed, creating a formula that would allow the shoe to appeal to a wider audience.

If that wasn't enough, the exposed Air unit harnessed the idea and success of the Air Max 1 (see pages 56–7) to create a shoe that was, and still is, coveted and revered by Air Jordan fanatics across the globe.

Opposite: The Air Jordan III was an innovative basketball shoe design and the first shoe in the Air Jordan line to display the now-iconic Jumpman logo

In 1989 adidas built on its already popular ZX line, first launched with the '00 series in 1984, by introducing the '000 series to the world. With the ZX '000 series, adidas took its technical running series to a whole new level by pioneering not only the company's new cushioning technology, Soft Cell, but also its now-famous stability technology, Torsion.

Not quite the most technical shoe in the ZX '000 range (that title goes to the ZX 9000), the ZX 8000 was nonetheless by far the most striking. With a silhouette almost identical to the ZX 9000 and a teal colourway that was a lot brighter than any other ZX '000 model (or previous ZX '00 model), the ZX 8000 caught the attention of the running community and sneaker lovers almost instantly. The ZX line was all about technological advancement and futuristic design, and it was the ZX 8000 with its quasi-metallic, space-age aesthetic that embodied this to the maximum. Having been loved by sneaker fans for decades, the ZX 8000 has remained a classic, with its distinctive shape, colourway and mix of materials all contributing to its iconic status.

Not only did the ZX 8000 and its new technologies influence running culture and the future of adidas's running shoes, it also went on to be the main influence for one of the most important shoe designs for the adidas Originals brand in 2014 – the ZX Flux (see pages 120–21).

It's hard to believe but the original archive pair of ZX 8000 (opposite) once popped like the bright reissues pictured below.

# adidas
# ZX 8000

**1989**

# Nike
# Air Jordan IV

**1989**

With the enthusiasm for Air Jordan shoes encouraged by the premium appeal of the Air Jordan III (see pages 62–3), the Air Jordan IV offered more from a performance standpoint. Although the shoe wasn't as revolutionary as the III, the design focused on refining the performance attributes. The plastic-mesh overlays, plastic heel support and lockdown lacing system provided a more responsive shoe. Nike's Flight line was closely associated with the IV, which was part of a bigger spectrum of Flight basketball designs released in 1989.

That's not to say that the Air Jordan IV didn't have style and cultural appeal, too. In its marriage of art and science, it was a sign of things to come from Nike in the field of basketball footwear design. The design of the IV still continues to be the preferred model for many, with the white/cement and black versions as revered as they were the first time around. The reissue of the white/cement version in 1999 sparked a retro craze that carried over into the new millennium.

Combine all of that with the provocative Mars Blackmon (a fictional character from Spike Lee's 1986 film *She's Gotta Have It*) ad campaigns by Wieden+Kennedy and you have a recipe for success. The appeal of the Air Jordan IV white/cement was further solidified through the legendary 'buggin' out' scene from another Spike Lee film, *Do the Right Thing* (1989), which played on the obsession for having the latest Air Jordans.

Opposite:
To this day the Air Jordan IV remains a firm favourite among collectors and Air Jordan fans.

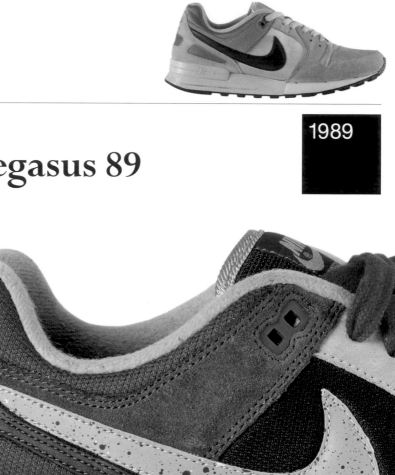

# Nike
# Air Pegasus 89

1989

The Nike Air Pegasus line was originally launched in 1983, but it was this version from 1989 that has evolved into a style icon. Although the 1983 original is a style classic, and the Pegasus line has gone on to produce countless style champions such as the Racer, the 1992 or the Pegasus 30, none of them quite beats this 1989 version.

The Pegasus line was Nike's dominant running offering throughout the 1980s, only to be surpassed eventually by the Air Max line that arrived in 1987 (see pages 56–7). The design of the Air Pegasus 89 doesn't actually differ that much from the Air Pegasus 1987 or Air Pegasus 1988 (Nike's best-selling shoe of that year), but in 1989 Nike perfected the design and introduced the iconic colourways that the Air Pegasus 89 is now known for.

The sharp shape of this shoe both on and off the foot has helped contribute to its long-lasting popularity, along with its reasonable price tag and durability, making it a popular choice for vintage Nike running fans. The combination of mesh and suede on the upper, teamed with a synthetic-leather Swoosh and the sharp midsole shape, make this shoe feel premium without losing its sporting edge.

Opposite: The Pegasus line is an unsung hero from Nike. The 1989 model has gained most recognition, with special make-ups such as the Berlin Wall from 2009 (main picture).

**Pump it up here.**

Released in 1989, the Reebok Pump was the result of a design collaboration between Reebok's Paul Litchfield and industrial design studio Design Continuum. The Reebok Pump was the first shoe to conceal an internal inflation system. Initially, the high selling price of the shoe and the success of Reebok's principal competitor, Nike, would delay the Reebok Pump's success story. However, the combination of NBA star Dominique Wilkins's endorsement, the Boston Celtics star Dee Brown's memorable 1991 NBA Slam-Dunk Contest win where he 'pumped' the sneakers before approaching the basket, and the allure of Reebok's Pump technology would allow the Pump line to achieve iconic status.

The Pump technology used inflatable chambers that pumped up for a custom fit and superior cushioning – an important and functional design element for basketball players. A high-rising tongue with the orange Pump logo was the source of the pumping action. Various ad campaigns would help the Reebok Pump to compete with Nike's Air technology – the 'Pump up and Air out!' Reebok tagline threw down a direct challenge to Nike and Michael Jordan. The brand would continue the Pump series with designs such as the Pump Omni, Omni Zone and Court Victory. Japanese streetwear enthusiasts paid particular attention to the Insta Pump Fury, giving the shoe a cult status.

Opposite and below: The bold aesthetics of the Reebok Pump made it easy to distinguish both on and off the court. The Pump system would go on to be the basis for a whole line of sneakers, not only in basketball (see overleaf).

# Reebok Pump

1989

**Basketball. The Omni Zone.**

Men's and Women's. THE PUMP™ System's air bladder offers the ultimate fit and an amazing degree of ankle support for a ¾-cut shoe. Combine this with the spring-like property of the ERS™ System, and you've got yourself a pair of shoes that will rise to any occasion.

**Basketball. Twilight Zone.**

Men's only. One of the most advanced performance basketball shoes. It combines THE PUMP™ full bladder system for a customized fit and extra ankle support with the ERS™ System for extra stability and shock absorption. Crucial stuff for smoother take-offs and landings.

**Cross Training. THE PUMP™ A**

Men's and Women's. The AXT Cr Trainer's infinitely adjustable fit bined with the lightweight cushio provided by Hexalite technology m this pair of shoes perfect for whate punishment you want to put ther (or yourself) through.

**Cross Training. THE PUMP™ SXT.**
Men's only. Although this shoe is built to take on any sport, its customized fit is especially helpful for those who spend more time weight training. The Mid-foot Stability Bar is designed to keep your foot from giving in to the pressure overhead.

**Tennis. THE PUMP™ Court Victory.**
Men's only. With the inflatable air bladder you not only get a perfect fit, you get an amazing degree of lateral and medial support for all those quick stops and side-to-side starts. Together with Hexalite technology for lightweight cushioning and Dura Trac Plus for glue-like traction, you'll always be right where you need to be. On the ball.

**Aerobics. THE PUMP™ Aerobic Lite**
Women's only. Whether you're into high-impact or low-impact, you can adjust THE PUMP to support you through any level of aerobics. While the lightweight Hexalite cushioning system will help absorb the shocks. How the rest of your body feels is up to you.
*Available in October 1990.

*The revolutionary PUMP™ technology is now available from $90.00.*

In 1990 Nike released the third design in the Air Max line, the Air Max III (in 2000 renamed the 'Air Max 90'). Its designer, Tinker Hatfield, once again used colour to draw attention to the technological advancements found within the shoe. A bright TPU panel surrounded the visible Air unit, but this time Hatfield spread the colour further throughout the design, using it to emphasize the branding on the side, rubber tread on the front of the outsole and the multi-lace port system on the upper. The Air Max 90 also introduced one of Nike's most iconic colours to the market – Infrared, a colour that has become strongly attached to Nike, to the 1990s and to this shoe in particular.

The Air Max 90 became a style icon in its own right, especially in the UK where it was as good as a uniform for the youth of the 1990s. Today it still remains one of the most enduring shoe designs, seeing regular colourways and reissues that keep it on our shelves and on our feet. It's worth mentioning that this shoe looks great all the way down to women's sizes, making it a popular choice for both sexes – a fact that undoubtedly contributes to its popularity.

Opposite: The Air Max 90 remains one of Nike's and Tinker Hatfield's best-loved designs. To this day, it is often remixed with new technologies and innovations.

75

# Nike
# Air Max 90

1990

# adidas
# EQT Running
# Cushion

1991

In 1991 adidas released the EQT line and changed the brand's future for ever. The EQT (or Equipment) range was much more than a new product or technology for adidas; it introduced a whole new perspective for the brand.

Along with EQT came a new performance logo for adidas, which marked the beginning of the end of the Trefoil in the world of sports performance. From 1997 the Trefoil would be dedicated solely to heritage products, becoming the icon for the adidas Originals subbrand in 2001.

The adidas EQT line was aimed at bringing adidas back to its roots in performance and was conceptualized and designed by the ex-Nike duo Rob Strasser (marketing) and Peter Moore (design), working through their new Sports Inc. agency. They also had the help of adidas's Jacques Chassaing (the man behind the ZX 500 – see pages 48–9 – and ZX 8000 – see pages 64–5). The bright colourful aesthetics of the 1980s and the ZX line were replaced with whites, greys and greens, giving the EQT line a clean and military functionality in its design language that made it stand out at the time and which is still remarkable today.

The adidas EQT Running Cushion was part of the original Running offering from the EQT line in 1991 and was designed as a supportive shoe for runners (hence the name). Using the same Torsion technology introduced by the ZX '000 range in 1989 (see pages 64–5), the EQT Running Cushion symbolizes one of the most important moments in adidas history and has become a classic both loved and hated by fans of the brand – some people simply weren't happy to see the Trefoil removed.

Opposite: The adidas EQT line was more than new product – it was a new way of thinking for adidas performance as a whole.

ASICS originally released the Gel Lyte III in 1991, at a time when running shoe designs were continuing to gain more and more popularity. It was reissued in 2006. The shoe's unique design features a split-tongue system that allows the shoe to fit more like a sock. The original colourways came in a variety of neon and pastel hues and utilized a mix of suede, nylon and mesh.

The Gel Lyte III provided unprecedented comfort, and its unique spit-tongue design worked with the lacing system to provide a locked-down fit for extra stability and support. ASICS's innovative Gel support system had been introduced in the 1980s, when it revolutionized the brand's footwear line. Its ability to absorb shock and impact was, and continues to be, popular among running enthusiasts.

Through an array of new colourways and reissues, the appetite and appreciation for the Gel Lyte III grew stronger in the latter half of the 2000s. The shoe was also a focal point in collaborations between ASICS and independent footwear stores. Some of the best results were achieved by SneakerFreaker, Alife, Concepts and Solebox. All provided a platform for the Gel Lyte III, to gain more attention within the sneaker community. However, it was the frequent collaboration projects with Ronnie Fieg (of KITH) – and their mesmerizing results – that catapulted the Gel Lyte III into the spotlight and solidified its iconic status within the sneaker collecting community.

Opposite: The ASICS Gel Lyte III offered unprecedented comfort for a running shoe and has received avid attention from recent sneaker collectors.

# ASICS
# Gel Lyte III

1991

A string of collaborations with Ronnie Fieg has propelled the Gel Lyte III to super-stardom in the sneaker and streetwear worlds.

# Nike
# Air Huarache

1991

The introduction of the Nike Huarache line in 1991 saw star designer Tinker Hatfield design a shoe that had, according to the original advertising copy, a 'typically Nike anything-goes design'. If Tinker had tried to be revolutionary with his design for the Air Max 1 (see pages 56–7), he outdid himself with the Air Huarache. Gone was the heel of the shoe, replaced with a thermoplastic strap; gone, too, was the Swoosh and the Nike Air logo. The Air Huarache was a wilfully strange beast and almost didn't make it to market for that very reason.

Inspired by the wetsuits used in water skiing, the lightweight blend of neoprene, Lycra and synthetic leather on the upper was instantly eye-catching. Its unusual looks were also due to colours that might have looked more at home in a science lab (although in fact they were inspired by the 1989 Nike Air Flow) as well as to the triangular shape of the overall silhouette, mirrored in the design of the Phylon midsole. The Air Huarache looked like a shoe from the future.

Along with its forward-thinking and attention-seeking design, the Air Huarache had an equally bold advertising campaign that asked runners 'HAVE YOU HUGGED YOUR FOOT TODAY?', putting emphasis on the *feel* of the shoe's unique design. The Air Huarache and its technologies were an instant success and achieved appreciation beyond the running fraternity, becoming popular in other sports, as well as outside of sports. Many bought the Air Huarache for its comfort and style alone (honourable mention to Jerry Seinfeld for wearing the Scream Green Air Huarache on TV in 1991).

The Air Huarache made history when Nike collaborated with a streetwear brand for the first time, creating the Stüssy x Nike Air Huaraches in 2000, arguably opening the door for streetwear collaborations at the brand. In more recent years, the Air Huarache has enjoyed a near-frenzied resurgence in popularity that has seen it even eclipse the Air Max line as a fashion icon.

Opposite: The shoe that nearly never happened: the Air Huarache had the people at Nike worried.

One of the stranger Air Max models from Nike – mainly because the brand chose not to include 'Max' in its name even though it was part of the Air Max line – the Nike Air 180 is yet another iconic Nike shoe from the early 1990s.

Released in 1992, sitting between the Air Max BW and Air Max 270 (aka Air Max 93), the Nike Air 180 was able to show off 180 degrees of its heel Air unit thanks to the addition of a clear panel in the outsole (the same Air unit seen in the Air Force 180 of the same year). The Air 180 also incorporated an inner sock system more akin to the Huarache line that had launched in 1991 (see pages 82–3), something that wouldn't be fully brought into the Air Max line until the Air Max 93. The 180-degree Air unit was brought to the Air Max line via the Air 180 and subsequently left the Air Max line when the Air 180 was discontinued, only one year after its launch. For many collectors the Air 180 became 'the-shoe-that-got-away', and it took Nike almost 15 years to finally reissue it (renaming it the Air Max 180).

The Air 180 was another of Tinker Hatfield's great designs and saw him harness the impact of colour to focus the viewer's attention on the shoe's refreshingly minimal aesthetics. For most of the original Air 180 colourways, the only colour found in the vast landscape of white was surrounding the Air unit, adorning the Swoosh and highlighting other branding at the rear of the shoe, thus emphasizing its sharp silhouette.

Opposite: The hugging form of the Air 180 makes it one of the best-fitting running shoes of all time.

# Nike
# Air 180

1992

# Vans
# Half Cab

With the Vans Caballero in 1989, Vans once again changed the game in skateboarding, creating the first pro skate shoe named after a skater – original Bones Brigade member Steve Caballero.

Super high for stability when skating vert ramp, the Vans Caballero was very much a product of its time. As skateboarding continued to evolve and kids started stepping out of the ramps in favour of skating the streets, they started to literally chop off the top of the Vans Caballero, sealing them with duct-tape and creating a mid-top version of the shoe to give them more mobility. Spotting what was going on, Steve Caballero tried the method out for himself and loved it. In 1992 Vans released the second Steve Caballero pro-model shoe, the Vans Half Cab, creating one of the most successful and iconic skate shoes of all time.

Outside of skateboarding, the Vans Half Cab has enjoyed an enviable position as a classic in streetwear culture, still remaining one of the most beloved shoes among the more discerning sneaker lovers. Skaters and streetwear fans love the grassroots story of the Half Cab so much that in 2012 Supreme and Vans released a version that was chopped in half and duct-taped as a homage to those who took it upon themselves to change the shoe (and Vans) back in the 1990s. To this day, the Half Cab remains a firm classic of the Vans offering as well as of skate culture.

Opposite: The Half Cab was invented by the consumer and put into production by the brand. A rare occurrence.

As street skating became ever more popular, skateboarding shoes had to adapt and the Half Cab became a streetwear icon.

Building on the success and technology of earlier New Balance running models, the 1500 marked a big development in the brand's running line. Released in 1993, the 1500 balanced technology and style. Like many earlier New Balance models, the shoe was available in a variety of materials with a mix of leather, suede, Nubuck and mesh. Its shape, colourways and style proved to be popular among collectors and would answer the demand for retro running designs executed to a high standard.

Throughout the 2000s the sneaker collecting world witnessed a huge amount of collaborations between brands and independent shoe stores across the globe. One of the most notable shoe designs to be used for collaboration projects was the New Balance 1500. The shoe became a beacon of sneaker authenticity and style for collectors. Many outstanding collaborations were produced, including designs by Solebox, Hanon, Provider, Crooked Tongues, Colette, Nice Kicks, Norse Projects, nonnative and Undefeated.

Reissues in the UK and Japan, along with the huge number of collaborations and limited-edition releases, sparked curiosity and interest for more of New Balance's 1990 running designs, and since then many other models have been reissued.

Opposite and below: Abetted by an array of outstanding collaborations during the 2000s, the New Balance 1500 was able to solidify its cult-like status among collectors.

# New Balance 1500

1993

# Nike
# Air Max 95

1995

Taking inspiration from the human body, Nike Air Max 95 designer Sergio Lozano took the Air Max line in a completely new direction. The shoe's overlaying materials resemble the human body in its structure. The design of the Air Max 95 builds up like the human anatomy, with the spine, muscles, ribcage and skin all represented in the layered materials. Nike's aim to channel the magical workings of nature was encapsulated in this design.

Not only was the Air Max 95 revolutionary, the appearance of the shoe was also a major factor in its popularity. The black/neon yellow combination created a shoe unlike any other Air Max before. It was another refreshing take on how a running shoe could look, with the neon accents emphasizing design attributes such as the Air units in the forefoot and heel areas.

The shoe re-established an appetite among fans for Nike's alluring Air Max technology. The great success of the Air Max 95 left people wondering how Nike could successfully follow the design, though the Air Max 97 (see pages 96–7) quickly achieved that. Like the Air Max Plus (see pages 100–101), the Air Max 95 achieved iconic status in more urban environments, finding sympathetic audiences among music and fashion countercultures. Those links stay strong to this day.

More than 150 colourways of the Air Max 95 have been produced over the years, allowing the popularity of the shoe to grow bigger and bigger. Experimentation with other materials, 360 Air units and further high-profile collaborations on the shoe have established the Air Max 95 as a style classic.

Opposite and below: Inspired by the human body, the unique design of the Nike Air Max 95 signified a bold change for the famous Air Max running line.

The Air Jordan signature line continued to be a success, but when Michael Jordan retired at the end of the 1994 NBA season many questioned whether or not the shoes would ever be the same again. Cue the Air Jordan XI.

Tinker Hatfield's most acknowledged design aside from the Air Max 1 (see pages 56-7), the Air Jordan XI couldn't have come at a more perfect time. Along with the return of Jordan in the 1995–6 NBA season came the Air Jordan XI, a design that looked and felt way ahead of its time. The performance aspect of the shoe harnessed the latest technological developments including a full-length Air sole unit, carbon-fibre plate and a design-savvy patent-leather and mesh upper. It was minimal but practical. While the shoe might not have yet have reached its full potential, it was nonetheless proof enough that this particular approach to designing basketball shoes was the future.

Like other Air Jordans before, the XI had cultural relevance, too. The Warner Bros 1996 film *Space Jam*, which starred Michael Jordan himself, played a huge part in the shoe's success and its wider appeal to an audience outside the realms of basketball and collectors. With Michael Jordan's growing popularity worldwide, the stage couldn't have been set more perfectly for the Air Jordan XI. To this day, the shoe retains its essence and allure and continues to be appreciated by old and new collectors alike. The 'Space Jam', 'Bred' and 'Concord' colourways still prove extremely popular among collectors and in the fashion world.

Opposite: Many variations of the Air Jordan XI have been created over the years, including the 'Space Jam', 'Concord' and 'Cool Grey' colourways.

95

# Nike
# Air Jordan XI

1996

# Nike
# Air Max 97

In 1997 Christian Tresser designed the first Air Max shoe to have an Air unit running the entire length of the shoe. The sleek, organic design of this shoe was inspired by Japan's high-speed Bullet trains, an inspiration that ran from the shape of the shoe through to the colour palette, with its metallic-silver aesthetic. A mixture of 3M and mesh on the upper gave the shoe a futuristic look that was a natural step forward from the Air Max 95 (see pages 92–3), a trick that Nike missed when designing the much lesser-known Air Max 96. Following the Air Max 95 was always going to be a struggle, but with the Air Max 97 Nike finally had a successor.

Thanks to its sleek shape and sweeping lines designed to inspire motion (as well as, of course, its vast amount of Air), the Air Max 97 became yet another iconic hit for Nike and the Air Max line, especially in Europe. Youth cultures in the UK, France and Italy, in particular, adopted the Air Max 97 as their own and it has remained a style classic within these groups ever since.

Considering its success, the Air Max 97 has gone on to be produced in a relatively small number of colourways (though at least it has remained on the shelves, unlike Christian Tresser's other 1997 masterpiece, the Zoom Air Spiridon). However, a few notable mashups and technological innovations include the Air Max 97/360, 'Vac Tech', 'Engineered Mesh' and 'Hyperfuse'.

Opposite: Inspired by a distinctly Japanese aesthetic, the Air Max 97 found its home in Europe, where it was adopted by urban youth.

Part of Nike's innovative and futuristic approach to design in the 1990s, the Air Foamposite One was designed by Eric Avar and was one of the first shoes to combine Nike's Foamposite technology and synthetic leather, signifying a dramatic change in the way materials and aesthetics worked together on a shoe.

The design took both visual and functional cues from a beetle's protective shell, and so the original colourway was a striking royal-blue/black combination. The appeal of the Air Foamposite One from a basketball players' point of view was that with continuous use the hardshell exterior softened and created a custom mould of the foot that acted as a support system for extreme lateral movements. This was, and continues to be, revolutionary stuff.

The Air Foamposite One is most closely associated with Orlando Magic star Anfernee Deon 'Penny' Hardaway and, although not an official signature shoe, paved the way for designs such as the Little Penny Posite. In the United States the Air Foamposite One was revered, but on UK soil most just gasped at the mere sight of them. Today, however, things are a little different. Along with the current boom in popularity of Air Jordan and other basketball shoes, the Air Foamposite One has slowly gained a new-found appreciation in UK fashion movements. Some shoes are distinctly American in their style and the Air Foamposite One is a prime example.

Although this controversial design continues to split opinion, it firmly stands as an iconic design that broke the mould of traditional material application and aesthetics and was unapologetic in doing so.

# Nike
# Air Foamposite One

1997

# Nike
# Air Max Plus

1998

The Nike Air Max Plus, or the 'TN' (Tuned 1) as many people know it, was a firm favourite in London and across the UK. The TN's success and iconic status in the UK began with the shoe's popularity in the London garage and grime music scenes of the late 1990s. That association led to an influx of street-savvy teenagers and young adults all revering the Air Max Plus. Its success extended across Europe into other urban areas including Paris, where the shoe would receive similar appreciation. It even resonated as far as Australia, but didn't achieve the same success in the United States. Along with its iconic status in the garage and grime circles in London, the Nike Air Max Plus would also garner appreciation in the graffiti subculture.

The Air Max Plus was an outstanding technical running shoe and exemplified Nike's late-1990s period of experimentation, which built on the innovative design of the Air Max 95 (see pages 92–3), Air Max 97 (see pages 96–7) and Air Max 98. The gradient uppers of the TN were revelatory and the new cushioning system reinforced the allure of Nike's Air technology. The 'OG Hyper Blue' and 'Orange Tiger' variations still stand as some of the best colourways ever. With the bold colour gradient aesthetics, it was the beginning of Nike's new approach to colour application and a taste of things to come over the following decade.

Opposite and below: The Air Max Plus became a must-have in certain subcultures. Original colour-ways featured striking colour fades across the upper.

101

Designed by Tobie Hatfield (Tinker Hatfield's younger brother), the Air Presto released in 2000 to usher in a new millennium and a return to super-minimalism in design, which hadn't been seen at Nike since the late 1980s with the Sock Racer, Air Sock and Air Flow. The Air Presto was part of Nike's Alpha Project of the late 1990s, a project that utilized statement-level technology across all of their categories, signified by the five dots found on the outsole of the Air Presto.

The Air Presto was revolutionary in its thinking on every level – a sock upper with added support provided by an engineered cage lacing system was complemented by a reinforced toecap to create the now iconic shape of the silhouette. Even how the shoes were sized ran against the norm, inspired by T-shirt sizing and ranging from XXS to XL. Colourways were deliberately eye-catching and often included printed designs on the sock-like upper that were well ahead of the times – something that has recently been brought back into fashion by the adidas originals ZX Flux (see pages 120–21). Thankfully for Nike, the Presto wasn't too ahead of its time and its modernistic style was picked up by both runners and those who appreciated the Air Presto as a casual sneaker.

Having designed the Air Rift in 1995, as well as Michael Johnson's Gold Shoe in 1996, Tobie Hatfield was dedicated to reducing the restriction running shoes imposed on the foot, a path that would eventually lead him to designing the Nike Free (see pages 104–5). However, it was the Nike Air Presto that was the first major commercial success for this minimalist approach.

Opposite: A lot of what the Presto represented wouldn't become popular in mass culture for at least another decade.

# Nike
# Air Presto

2000

First released in 2004, the Nike Free 5.0 epitomized the idea of barefoot running that Nike had been building on (not always successfully) and which it now presented to a mainstream audience. It was quickly accepted in the athletic and fashion worlds. Originally engineered by Tobie Hatfield and Eric Avar, the Nike Free was the result of eight years of research and was a landmark design for the brand.

The shoe was initially released with a numbering system that indicated the cushioning system in place, ranging from 0 (barefoot) to 10 (normal running shoe) – hence the Free 3.0, 5.0 and 7.0 variations, with 3.0 being the least cushioned and 7.0 the most. The synthetic suede upper provided stability and support and was combined with the breathability of the neoprene and nylon mesh panelling.

The design was quickly adopted by collectors and Nike fanatics, who hailed the shoe as one of the more outstanding modern releases. In 2006 it even won recognition in the form of a Stüssy x Nike Free Trail 5.0. As Nike's Free technology developed in tandem with other innovative materials from the brand, 2010 saw the release of the Nike Free Run+. This built on the design prowess of the original Nike Free and also modernized the aesthetics. Later, Nike introduced the Nike Free Run+ 2. This is where the major shift in the public perception of the technical running shoe took place. From then on, the sneaker world, fashion world and general public became more interested in the modern running aesthetic that Nike was producing.

Opposite: The Nike Free 5.0 was a pinnacle design for the brand, changing the way shoe design was approached over the next decade.

# Nike Free 5.0

2004

# Gourmet
# Quadici

Launched in 2006, Gourmet is without a doubt one of the more interesting and experimental sneaker brands of recent history, doing its best to combine different cultures and influences in all that it does. Although not one of the launch models and not necessarily the shoe it is most widely known for today, the Quadici was the shoe that garnered the brand the most attention in its earlier years.

A mashup of a duck boot, chukka and running shoe, the Quadici was a brave move at a time when sneakers weren't terribly adventurous, though it turned out to be a success. Early models were almost always made in tonal colourways, with an offering of either traditional muted greens and browns or more vibrant modern teals and oranges. The crisp white midsole with its oversized air unit gave what was otherwise a very formal-looking and premium shoe a sporting edge, making it a very versatile silhouette to style.

The Quadici has since gone on to be updated into the Quadici Lite, but it's this original version that will be remembered as the shoe that finally woke people up (especially in Europe) to Gourmet – and all thanks to Greg Lucci's bold approach to design.

Opposite and below: The air bubble and duck boot detailing of the Quadici is a perfect representation of the Gourmet brand and its love of culture clash.

The Nike Air Yeezy project saw Nike collaborating with world-renowned hip-hop artist Kanye West. After months of doubt surrounding the release, the project came to fruition in 2009 and turned up the heat on the sneaker collecting frenzy.

It's almost crazy to think that the £160 ($245) price tag of the original Nike Air Yeezy seems pretty reasonable today, but at the time it was almost as steep as they came. The media storm surrounding the release was at a level unseen for sneakers prior to this, partly thanks to Kanye West's already established reputation as a controversial rapper and hip-hop producer. The Air Yeezy was one of the biggest collaborations on a sports shoe to date.

The Air Yeezy displayed West's design skills, with the shoe taking cues from several Nike classics, including the Air Jordan III (see pages 62–3) and Air Jordan V. It was a design that utilized familiar Nike design elements and infused them with a contemporary twist. The Nike Air Yeezy was the result of Kanye West's creative vision and Nike's rich history of design innovation. In that respect, it was destined to be a hit among sneaker collectors, fashionistas and those with creative inclinations.

The Nike Air Yeezy was soon to be followed up by the Nike Air Yeezy II in 2012 and the controversial Nike Air Yeezy II 'Red October' in 2014. Both sneakers would achieve unprecedented levels of attention.

Opposite: The Nike Air Yeezy caused an unprecedented hype. Air Yeezys and Air Yeezy IIs still fetch huge prices on the second-hand market.

# Nike
# Air Yeezy

2009

# Nike
# SB Zoom
# Stefan Janoski

2009

Released at a time when vintage vulcanized skate shoes like the Vans Authentic (see pages 16–17) and Era were beginning a resurgence in popular culture, Nike SB released its first pro model from Stefan Janoski – the Nike SB Zoom Stefan Janoski.

Pared-back, vulcanized, canvas shoes have always had their place in skateboarding, and at the time skaters were opting to go simple again, so it made sense that the Zoom Stefan Janoski would do well in the skateboarding world. However, it was the popularity it quickly gained *outside* the world of skateboarding that was so interesting.

Nike SB managed to time it right and found itself riding the crest of a wave of popularity that saw the Zoom Stefan Janoski fly off the shelves. Whole new customer bases opened up to skate stores over the next few years as both skate shoes and sneakers in general became more and more popular beyond their normal markets. The Zoom Stefan Janoski was pretty hard not to like the look of and was as simple as using an iPod when it came to styling it into an outfit (unlike a lot of the more technical sports shoes). Its minimal, yet honed, aesthetic made it as smart as it was casual. As the general public relaxed its look in general, the Zoom Stefan Janoski became a go-to choice and has remained one ever since.

Opposite: The Nike SB Zoom Stefan Janoski marks the moment where Nike SB truly broke both the skateboarding and lifestyle markets.

The Nike LeBron signature line already had six designs under its belt before it really gained any widespread attention. With the release of the LeBron VII ending up turning heads in sneaker collecting circles, the anticipation for the eighth instalment was more enthusiastic than before.

The Nike LeBron 8 was a defining shoe in the signature line, owing to LeBron James's transfer to Miami Heat in the summer of 2010. However, there were various design attributes that made this design stand out from those before it. The LeBron 8 intelligently blended premium materials and high-performance technology. LeBron's signature shoes tended to make heavy use of technologies such as full-length 360 Air units and Flywire, with the LeBron 8 combining those two technologies with premium leather and suede panelling. A range of various colourways also had appeal for a wider audience. It was a design that played to the interests of LeBron James's style of play and also to the tastes of sports shoe fans and collectors worldwide.

Since the LeBron 8, the designer of the signature line, Jason Petrie, has developed the series into something special and memorable. Many would argue that the Nike LeBron 9 and 10 are the better-looking shoes now. However, the LeBron 8 was the design that initiated the lifestyle crossover, solidifying the LeBron signature line as a legitimate off-court choice and style icon.

Opposite: The Nike LeBron 8 was released soon after LeBron's departure from the Cleveland Cavaliers to Miami Heat.

113

# Nike LeBron 8

2010

The *Miami Vice*-style colourway of the LeBron 8 boldly announced the player's commitment to his newly adopted city.

# Nike
# Flyknit Trainer

Not only was the Nike Flyknit Trainer a technological shoe for runners; instantly it had lifestyle and fashion appeal. With the Nike Free technology (see pages 104–5) already established and appreciated by athletes, sports shoe fans and fashionistas, the Flyknit Trainer was the perfect follow-up to that initial desire for technical running shoes with minimalist aesthetics.

Emphasizing only the essential design elements for optimal running performance, the Flyknit Trainer is a showcase for the art of minimalism. The design featured a featherweight structure and an intelligent woven support system that had never been seen before, acting like a sock and shaping to the foot. Along with that, the environmentally friendly one-piece upper doesn't use multiple layers of materials to construct the shoe.

This considered execution resulted in the fashion- and design-conscious communities choosing the Flyknit Trainer for their everyday shoe. Its elegant aesthetics and vivid colour options, including multicoloured variations, were right on time and had unisex appeal. Releasing just ahead of the 2012 London Olympics, the bright Flyknit Trainer was instantly recognizable on athletes. The 'Chukka' and 'Lunar' variations that followed further enhanced its reputation among collectors and fashion consumers, who gave the Flyknit project a collective nod of approval.

The Flyknit Trainer demonstrated Nike's innovative approach to design and style on a grand scale. It's a modern running shoe that successfully crosses the boundaries of performance and fashion.

Opposite: The innovative Flyknit Trainer channelled the benefits of Nike's advanced Flyknit technology and minimal aesthetics to great success.

In 2012 the Roshe Run silently entered the world and became a hit out of nowhere. When you learn about the inspirations behind the shoe, it can come as a surprise to discover that the Roshe Run now dominates the sneaker market.

Inspired by the meditation-based philosophy of Japanese Zen Buddhism, the Roshe Run takes its name from the Zen master's title while its design ethos is deeply rooted in the Japanese garden. The Roshe Run took Nike's approach of 'less is more' and attempted to do just enough. If the Air Presto (see pages 102–3) was a successful exercise in minimalism, the Roshe Run took things further, reducing complication even more (no easy feat).

The one-piece waffle outsole was reminiscent of the simplicity of the Nike Free 5.0 (see pages 104–5), but without the technology. The deconstructed mesh upper was sporty, yet casual, and had design cues similar to the structure of the highly successful Nike SB Zoom Stefan Janoski (see pages 110–11). The Roshe Run was neither masculine nor feminine; it didn't promise 'performance', but neither did it look useless; it wasn't cheap, nor was it expensive. It sat right in the middle of everything and people loved it for it.

As soon as it hit the shelves, it caused a frenzy as word spread about the new shoe, creating its own micro-trend in fashion – one that would inspire a shift in direction for other brands.

The Roshe Run had arrived, quietly and calmly, and it had changed everything.

Opposite: Quiet revolution: the success of the Roshe Run was predicted by few, but enjoyed by many.

# Nike
# Roshe Run

2012

# adidas
# Originals ZX Flux

2014

Taking one of adidas's all-time classics, the ZX 8000, from 1989 (see pages 64–5) and stripping it back as far as it could go, adidas Originals created the ZX Flux at the start of 2014.

Designed by Sam Handy, the ZX Flux was an attempt to modernize the running offering from adidas Originals while still retaining the subbrand's heritage and archive appeal, and it has proved a near-instant success. The ZX Flux marks the first time that adidas Originals has truly looked both to the past and to the future on a large scale, and it's this that's made the ZX Flux such an important milestone for the brand.

The super-fast-looking shape of the silhouette builds on what was already a speedy-looking sneaker in the form of the ZX 8000, but is here taken to taken it to a whole new level, helping the shoe appeal to a much wider range of people with its easy styleability. It is already clear that the approach to both the design and the release strategy of this sneaker is a pivotal moment for adidas Originals. The shoe has become an instant success, making it a definite icon of style for the future.

Constant experimentation, as seen in the printed versions that hark back to the style of the Nike Air Presto (see pages 102–3), and the mi ZX Flux Photo Print app that allows people to print their own photos on the upper of the shoe, has also helped to secure this sneaker's already-bright future.

Opposite and below: The beginning of the future for adidas Originals? The ZX Flux has already made a large impact in a small amount of time, and it's not slowing down.

# Index

126 Mitchell Beazley would like to acknowledge and thank all those who have kindly provided material for publication in this book.

Sneakers on pages 58, 59, 68 below, 98 and 108 kindly lent by Kish Kash from Soleheaven/Crepe City/ The All City Show.

Sneakers on pages 36 right, 80–81, 114–115 and 118 kindly lent by Ron Raichura from Crepe City.

Pages 2, 20 Laurence Watson/PYMCA; 8, 10-11, 12, 13 courtesy of Converse; 14, 36, 58, 59, 65, 68, 80-81, 98, 108, 110, 111, 114-5, 116, 118 Karl Adamson © Octopus Publishing Group; 15, 22, 23, 28, 29, 32, 33, 46, 47, 48, 64, 120, 121 courtesy of Adidas; 16, 30, 35, 86 courtesy of Vans; 18, 19 courtesy of PUMA; 24, 93, 102 right © Nike Inc.; 26, 40, 54, 56, 62, 74, 84, 92, 94, 96, 100, 101, 102 left © Rachael Cox – FootWorld; 34 Universal/ The Kobal Collection; 38 courtesy of Saucony; 42, 44, 70, 71, 72-73 courtesy of Reebok UK; 50 Andrew D. Bernstein/NBAE/Getty Images; 52-53 Focus on Sport/Getty Images; 60, 90, 91 courtesy of New Balance; 63, 66 Sunshining7 – Ruddy Sebban; 76, 82 © END; 78 courtesy of ASICS; 88-89 Sam Scott-Hunter/PYMCA/Rex Features; 104 courtesy of footlocker. eu; 106, 107 Gourmet Footwear www. gourmetfootwear.com; 112 Victor Baldizon/NBAE/Getty Images.

# Acknowledgements

An Hachette UK Company
www.hachette.co.uk

First published in Great Britain in 2015
by Mitchell Beazley, a division of
Octopus Publishing Group Ltd
Carmelite House
50 Victoria Embankment
London EC4Y 0DZ
www.octopusbooks.co.uk
www.octopusbooksusa.com

Distributed in the US by
Hachette Book Group
1290 Avenue of the Americas
4th and 5th Floors
New York, NY 10020

Distributed in Canada by
Canadian Manda Group
664 Annette St.
Toronto, Ontario, Canada M6S 2C8

ISBN 978 1 84533 995 1

A CIP catalogue record for this book
is available from the British Library

Printed and bound in China

10 9 8 7 6 5 4 3 2 1

Commissioning Editor:
Joe Cottington
Managing Editor:
Sybella Stephens
Editor:
Robert Anderson
Art Director:
Jonathan Christie
Design:
Untitled
Picture Researcher:
Sophie Hartley
Production Controller:
Sarah Kramer

# Credits

Founded in 2009, The Daily Street is one of the world's leading destinations for up-to-date news, reviews and features on men's fashion and lifestyle, from the biggest stories in streetwear to the latest news in music, art and live events.

Based in London, the TDS team work closely with brands and retailers – from small independent start-ups to global leaders – to bring together a curated edit of happenings in the streetwear world. Whether it's exclusive interviews with key industry names, commissioned videos and photo shoots, exclusive music content or articles covering everything from classic sneakers to news on the very latest releases, The Daily Street is one of the most highly respected voices in streetwear.

www.thedailystreet.co.uk

# About the author